I0199078

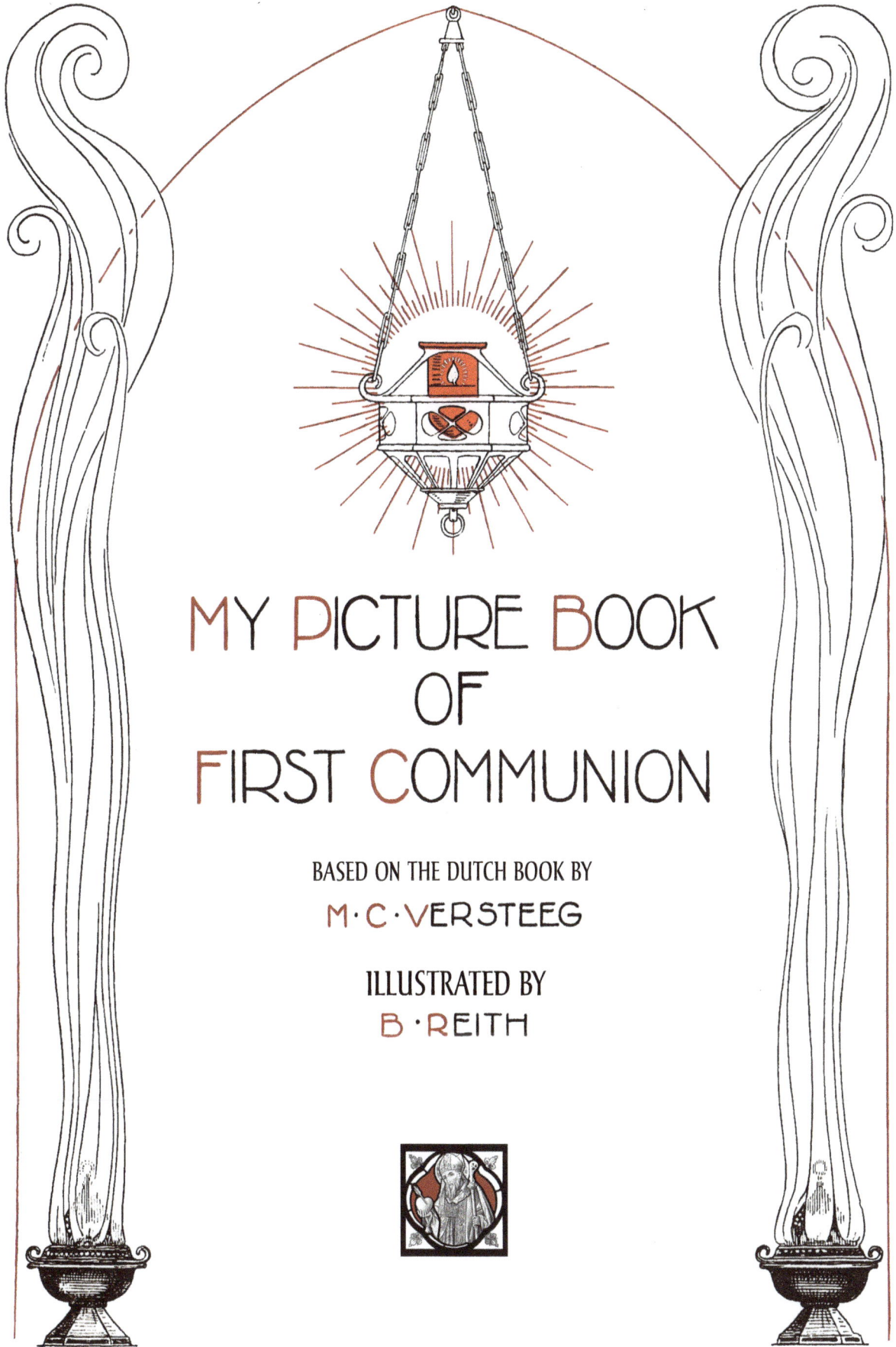

MY PICTURE BOOK
OF
FIRST COMMUNION

BASED ON THE DUTCH BOOK BY

M·C·VERSTEEG

ILLUSTRATED BY

B·REITH

· ST. AUGUSTINE ACADEMY PRESS · HOMER GLEN ·

·REITH·

PREPARING FOR FIRST HOLY COMMUNION

Here are James and Mary. They have recently received their First Holy Communion. There were many things they needed to learn in order to prepare. The most important things they learned were *who* comes to them in Holy Communion, and *why* He comes.

Now that you are preparing for your First Communion, James and Mary will help you to learn these things and prepare.

Let us begin here in the church.

IN THE CHURCH, ON THE ALTAR IS JESUS

Anytime we enter a church, we always show reverence. We genuflect and make the sign of the cross with holy water.

Why do we do this?

We do this because we know that the church is the house of God. It is a very holy place.

It is not like our house, where we eat and sleep and work and play. We come to church to worship God.

Look at the altar in this picture. What do you see? There, in the very center, is a special, sacred golden house called the tabernacle. Jesus is inside this golden house.

All of the things around the tabernacle are meant to tell us that Jesus is there. First, it is very beautiful. The altar top is dressed with fine, pure white cloths. There are candles. And there is always a crucifix to remind us of Jesus' sacrifice for us.

But do we see Jesus Himself? And can we see those angels there, bowing to their Lord and God? No, we can not see them. But we know they are there. The flame burning in the red sanctuary lamp reminds us that they are there. That is why James and Mary have learned to bow their heads and fold their hands in prayer when they approach the altar.

We do well to be like them when we enter the church. We will always remember to say a prayer and ask Jesus to bless us.

Even when we pass a church in the street, and do not enter, what a nice thing it is to bow our heads for a moment, remembering that Jesus lives within, and whisper a quick greeting to Him from our hearts!

Good morning, sweet Jesus, my Savior!
Good morning, dear Mary, my Queen!
Good morning, bright Angels, fair Guardians,
Of Jesus, Who dwells here unseen.

THE SACRED HOST IS JESUS

When we go to church for Mass or Benediction, there are many more things we can see that show how special God's house is.

When the priest is praying to God on behalf of the whole church, he wears special clothing called *vestments*. See the priest and the altar servers in this picture. The vestments they are wearing are very handsome, and different from the clothes we all wear. This is because they have special meaning and they give special honor to God.

When he approaches the tabernacle, the priest genuflects and bows his head. Then he opens the golden door reverently. Here at the bottom of the page you can see what he sees.

First, there is a delicate silk curtain called a veil. The priest pushes this aside and you can see that the inside of the tabernacle is covered with gold.

Inside this wonderful golden house is a beautiful vessel that is also covered with a veil. When this veil is removed, we can see that the vessel looks like a chalice with a lid. It is called a *ciborium,* and inside, it too is lined in either gold or silver.

We offer only the finest and most costly materials for those things which contain or touch our Lord.

When the priest removes the cover from the ciborium, do we see Jesus inside? No, we can not see Him — but He is there!

There inside the ciborium is the Sacred Host — and the Sacred Host is Jesus! Jesus is hidden in the Sacred Host.

The priest and the people know this well. The priest bows and genuflects before Jesus hidden here in the ciborium, and with care and devotion, he shows the Sacred Host to the people. They all kneel and show the greatest reverence for Jesus. That is just what the altar servers are doing here.

When we see Jesus in the Sacred Host, we give Him all our homage and love.

Sweetest Jesus, kind and dear,
For my sake abiding here,
Look on me who kneel before,
This your little curtained door.

Through that door if I could see,
Like bread you would look to me,
But You're truly there I know,
You, Yourself have told me so.

Hear me, Jesus, while I pray,
And guide me along earth's way,
Till the time when I shall see,
You in all Your Majesty.

JESUS IS IN THE SACRED HOST, TO COME INTO OUR HEARTS.

In ancient times, men bent their knees and made offerings and sacrifices to statues of their great and terrible gods. But we do not worship a statue.

We worship a living God, the God who created us and loves us. And when we go to Mass to give our worship to God, we do something very different than they did.

We too make offerings to God. We offer Him the sacrifice of His beloved Son in Holy Mass. Jesus Himself is our Sacrifice.

When the priest shows us Jesus in the Sacred Host, we give him our homage and reverence. But now see what the priest does with the Host at Mass!

The priest has come down from the altar. Here, at the edge of the Sanctuary, is the communion rail where the children in this picture are patiently kneeling. A fine white cloth covers the communion rail and the children place their hands under it and lift it close to them.

They do this to prepare for what comes next. See how the priest shows the Sacred Host to the girl.

What does he do next? He places the Sacred Host carefully on the girl's tongue. She lets it soften and gently swallows, so that it rests inside her, close to her heart.

Jesus is now dwelling, not in the beautiful golden house, but in the girl's heart! How happy she is!

And Jesus is happy too. That is why He comes to live in the tabernacle, hidden under the appearance of a little piece of bread. In this way, he can come directly into our hearts — by becoming our food!

Oh, what a wonderful mystery this is!

Jesus, Jesus, come to me,
Oh, how much I long for Thee!
Come Thou of all friends the best,
Take possession of my breast.

Comfort my poor soul distressed,
Come and dwell within my breast,
Oh, how oft I sigh for Thee,
Jesus, Jesus, come to me!

Empty is all worldly joy,
Ever mixed with some alloy,
I my heart, to Thee resign.
O what rapture to be Thine!

THE BREAD BECOMES THE SACRED HOST

Look at this page. We see two round, white pieces of bread. At first glance, they look the same. But they are different — let us see how.

At the bottom of the picture, we see how the beautiful wheat grows. It has a long, straight stem with narrow leaves, and at the top of the stem is a spike with many seeds. When these seeds dry and fall to the ground, they create new life by growing into a new stalk of wheat.

But those seeds also give us life when we eat them. We grind them into flour, and from the flour we make bread. From this wheat flour the special round white bread is made. But the bread at the bottom of the picture has not yet become the Sacred Host. It has not yet been *consecrated.*

During the Mass, the priest repeats Jesus' words from the Last Supper, when He took bread, blessed and broke it, and gave it to his disciples saying,

> "Take and eat of this, all of you… For this is My Body."

In that moment, when the priest speaks these words, the little round white piece of bread *truly becomes the body of our Lord Jesus Christ.*

But it still looks the same, does it not? And if you smell or taste it, it smells and tastes the same. When the priest breaks it, it breaks just the same.

But the Angels know the difference. See how they gather around and bow in homage, singing the song they sing in heaven: Holy Holy Holy is the Lord of hosts! *Hosanna in excelsis!*

Here the artist has shown the Sacred Host with beautiful golden rays shining all around. But our eyes cannot see the difference, and no artist can show us how beautiful and holy the Sacred Host truly is.

When Moses looked upon the face of God on Mount Sinai, it made his own face shine so brightly that he had to cover it with a veil so that the Israelites would not be blinded.

In the same way should we regard the Sacred Host: it is truly the most holy Body of our Lord Jesus Christ, and only the priest may now touch it, for his hands are consecrated too.

Jesus, Eternal God and King
Who made this world and everything,
How small Thou art within the Host,
Yet there, I think, I love Thee most,
Because it is to gain my heart
That Thou a little Prisoner art.

·REITH·

THE SACRED HOST IS DISPLAYED FOR WORSHIP

How fortunate we are to be Catholic! We know that our God loves us so dearly that He comes down from heaven to become our food, and enter into our hearts! And He does this in every Mass! Oh, how much He loves us!

Sometimes we just want to look at the things we love. And so in addition to the Mass, our Church has a special liturgy that we call *Benediction of the Blessed Sacrament*. Here, rather than receiving the Sacred Host in Holy Communion, we look upon the Sacred Host and we sing solemn hymns of praise to God before receiving His blessing.

During Benediction, the priest comes to the altar. He genuflects, opens the door of the tabernacle, and removes the Sacred Host from its beautiful golden home. He then places it in the center of a splendid golden throne made especially to hold the Host in Majesty. This special throne is called a *monstrance*. You can see two different kinds of monstrances on this page.

The priest then places the splendid monstrance upon the altar, high up where all can see. The servers ring the bell to alert us to look to Jesus and offer him our prayers and adoration. The priest puts incense in the censer and lets sweet-smelling clouds of incense rise to Jesus. The singers in the choir chant their hymns of adoration, the candles burn brightly, and the flowers offer their beauty and fragrance.

All for Thee, O Jesus!

When the hymns of praise are complete, the priest once more lifts the monstrance and makes a great sign of the cross over the people, blessing them in the name of the Father, and the Son, and the Holy Ghost.

Then the priest removes the Sacred Host from the monstrance and returns it to its beautiful golden home in the Tabernacle. Our service of Benediction is now complete.

> Oh Jesus truly hidden
> Within that Sacred Host,
> Who heaven's gates hast opened
> At such a bitter cost,
>
> Fierce foes surround us daily,
> Lord, shield us with thy care,
> From Heaven's heights defend us
> And bring us safely there.

REITH

WHO IS JESUS? JESUS IS GOD THE SON.

The best painter who ever lived cannot paint heaven. It is too wonderful for the best imagination. This is why the Bible tells us "Eye hath not seen, nor ear heard, …what things God hath prepared for them that love Him." (1 Cor 2:9)

Yet we like to try. This picture shows us a little glimpse of heaven, where God sits enthroned in majesty, surrounded by the angels who never rest, but are always singing "Holy, Holy, Holy!"

Who do we see here? We know that there is only one God. But we also remember from the Catechism that *in God there are Three Divine Persons*. That is what we see here: The Father, the Son and the Holy Ghost, who is shown in the form of a dove.

The picture below the clouds of heaven is very different. On the left, we see poor Adam and Eve being driven out of Paradise because they had disobeyed God. Their lives now will be hard and full of toil. They can never return.

On the right are the children of Adam and Eve: Moses, the Prophets and the people of God. They have inherited the sin of Adam and Eve, called *original sin*. They try to love and obey God, but they cannot come to heaven because it is closed to them. See how they weep and cry out to God. They beg to be saved.

God hears their cries, and loves them, and has pity on them. See how the Father and the Son look at one another. They gaze deeply into each other's eyes, with a gaze full of wisdom and love and compassion. The Will of the Father and the Will of the Son are one: God desires to save His people.

A single word or act might have atoned for our sin, but God's love is so great that He wants to do more. He will not merely save His people, He will live among them and teach them, and give them every example of holiness. From His throne in highest heaven He will come down low, not as an angel or a king, or even a rich man. Through the working of the Holy Spirit, he will be born as a tiny, helpless baby, to a poor carpenter and his young wife.

Our amazement and gratitude for this immense love is expressed in the solemn Easter Vigil Mass, when we speak of the sin of Adam and Eve, saying, "O happy fault that earned so great, so glorious a Redeemer!"

> O wonder of your humble care for us!
> O love, O charity beyond all telling,
> To ransom a slave you gave away your Son!
> O truly necessary sin of Adam,
> Destroyed completely by the Death of Christ!
> O happy fault
> That earned so great, so glorious a Redeemer!

AND THE WORD WAS MADE FLESH, AND DWELT AMONG US

You know the story of dear Jesus' birth. You hear it every year at Christmas...

How the angel Gabriel came to Mary and announced to her that she would bear God's Son...

How Mary and Joseph made the long journey to Bethlehem...

How the little Infant Savior was born there at midnight, in a lowly stable among the sheep and cattle...

And how the angels announced the wondrous birth to the simple shepherds, who came to find the scene we see here in this picture...

Compare this picture with the one on the previous page.

See now the throne that God has chosen for love of us: the radiant light of heaven has been replaced by darkness and cold.

The angels sing their hymn of glory from the skies, while the animals cry in surprise to find the newborn Lord of Heaven lying in their food-trough.

Yet Mary and Joseph know that this tiny, helpless babe is truly the great and powerful Creator of the universe, and they bow low in adoration and gratitude.

And oh, how wise is God! For even if we cannot understand this great mystery of how He loved us so well, yet who can resist loving a little baby! It is so easy to love the little Baby Jesus! Think how you would like to hold Him in your arms and cuddle Him.

> Dear little One! how sweet Thou art,
> Thine eyes how bright they shine,
> So bright they almost seem to speak,
> When Mary's look meets Thine.
>
> When Mary bids Thee sleep Thou sleep'st,
> Thou wakest when she calls;
> Thou art content upon her lap,
> Or in the rugged stalls.
>
> Joseph takes Thee in his arms,
> And smoothes Thy little cheek,
> Thou lookest up into his face,
> So helpless and so meek.
>
> Art Thou, weak Babe, my very God?
> Oh, I must love Thee then,
> Love Thee and yearn to spread Thy love
> Among forgetful men.

INRI

REITH.

GOD THE SON DIED ON THE CROSS

When we see the sweet little infant Jesus in the Manger at Christmas, it is easy to forget about Calvary and the sad scene we see here. Yes, Jesus became man so that He might teach us, not only by His Words, but also by His example. His whole life was one long journey toward Calvary.

He was a great King, yet he did not live in a palace with fine clothes and food and servants. No, he lived among us, *as one of us.* He was poor, and suffered cold in winter and heat in summer. He got cuts and scrapes and splinters and bruises, just like you do. He went hungry sometimes, and had his share of illness and loneliness. He had to work to help His mother in the house and His foster father in the workshop.

As He grew, we are told that he "advanced in wisdom, and age, and grace with God and men." He traveled from place to place, teaching in the synagogues and in the countryside. He healed the sick and the lame, and cured the deaf and the blind. But his greatest work was still to come.

So you see, Our Lord spent thirty years in His Hidden Life at Nazareth, giving us His example of how to live...

Then he spent three years in His Public Life teaching others and healing the sick...

Then he spent three hours in His Sacrifice for us, achieving our salvation.

Look at our Blessed Savior as he hangs on the cross for you and me. See the cruel crown of thorns, how it tears and disfigures his beautiful face. See the nails that pierce his hands — those hands that worked and prayed and healed. See the terrible wounds in His feet — those feet that carried him tirelessly from one end of the Holy Land to the other, preaching, teaching and blessing. See the droplets of Blood as they are poured out for us — slowly, slowly, to the last drop!

And to think that He suffered all this — *for you and me!* How we should hate sin, when we think how it disfigured our dear Lord, when we think how much He suffered to wash away all our sins so that the gates of heaven might once more be opened to us. Surely we must love Him very much, and when we see His Cross, we should kneel and thank him and tell Him we love Him.

O Jesus hanging on the Cross,
Look down on me your child.
I kneel before Thee sorrowing;
Your death my sins exiled.

I kiss thy wounds, hands, feet and side,
With faith, hope and charity;
O Jesus help me never more
To wander far from Thee.

JESUS INSTITUTES THE BLESSED SACRAMENT

By His death, Jesus opened the way to heaven for us, which had been closed by original sin. But He knew that we are like Adam and Eve: we fall so easily into temptation and sin. He could do His part, but we must also do our part by living well, praying well and avoiding sin, for only those without sin can enter heaven.

The strength and courage that we need to avoid sin is called *grace*. Now that Jesus had opened once more the way to heaven, God wanted us to have all the graces we need to come there. He gives us these graces in the *sacraments*.

The greatest of these sacraments Jesus gave us the night before He died. He would help us always to be good by being with us Himself — He would come directly into our hearts! How could he do this? Through a great miracle.

See Jesus in this picture. He is celebrating the sacred festival of the Passover with his disciples. It is a very special meal in which God's people recall when He delivered them out of slavery in Egypt. Now Jesus would deliver His people from slavery to sin.

All during this meal, the apostles have noticed that Jesus has been different.

He has knelt before them and humbly washed their feet.

He has told them the sad news that one of them would betray Him.

He has told them that He will be leaving them soon, and has done all things possible to prepare them for His departure.

He has poured out His Heart to them in a way that they have never seen before, and has drawn them all in love to Himself as if He would make them one with Him.

And while they were eating and speaking together, Jesus took the unleavened bread that was a customary part of the Passover meal, and, looking up to heaven, to God his Father, He said the blessing — and then He did something more. This was the great miracle! He said:

"Take and eat of this, all of you… For THIS IS MY BODY."

The apostles heard these words from Jesus with great wonder. Truly, this was no ordinary Passover. This was something new.

They knew who it was who had just told them, "THIS IS MY BODY." They could not understand it, but they knew he spoke the truth, and they believed Him.

Later, they would remember that He had told them:

"I am the living bread which came down from heaven. If any man eat of this bread, he shall live for ever; and the bread that I will give, is my flesh, for the life of the world... Amen, amen I say unto you: Except you eat the flesh of the Son of man, and drink his blood, you shall not have life in you." (John 6:51-54)

This was what He had meant. Here was the way in which God had planned from all eternity to be with us always. He would come from heaven, like manna, *to be our food*.

We cannot understand this great miracle, but Jesus has said it, so we know it is true and we believe.

Oh Jesus, I believe that you are truly present in the Sacred Host!

Jesus, Thou art coming, Holy as Thou art,
Thou the God who made me, to my sinful heart.
Jesus, I believe it, on Thy only word,
Kneeling I adore Thee, as my King and Lord.

THE COMMUNION OF THE APOSTLES

After Jesus had changed the bread into His body, He took the chalice of wine. Again He spoke the words of blessing that his disciples had heard in so many Passover celebrations. But once again Jesus began to say something new.

As He handed them the chalice, He said,

> "Drink of this, all of you, for THIS IS MY BLOOD of the new covenant, which will be poured out for you for the remission of sins."

What did this mean? The disciples understood what a covenant was. It is a very solemn promise between God and His people. They knew of God's covenants with Noah, with Abraham, with Moses, and with David. Each of these covenants was sealed with the sacrificial blood of animals.

Now Jesus was speaking of a *new* covenant sealed in His own blood, which would be shed on the cross the next day. But first He wanted to give to his beloved disciples two very great gifts of grace that they were to share with the whole world. These two great gifts were the first *sacraments*.

First Jesus would feed them with His own Body and Blood, establishing the sacrament of the *Eucharist*, so that He would be able to come into their hearts and stay with them and help them.

But he did not want to come into only *their* hearts. He wanted to come into *all of our hearts*. He wanted to stay near to each of us, and help us to be good and come to heaven. So He would make it possible for his disciples to repeat this gift of grace and share it with others until the end of time.

He did this by saying:

"Do this in remembrance of Me."

With these words, Jesus made *priests* of the twelve Apostles, giving them the ability to change bread and wine into His Body and Blood, so that He could come into the hearts of all mankind. This sacrament of the priesthood is called *Holy Orders*.

Look at this beautiful picture. See with what reverence the Apostles receive the most holy Body and Blood of their Lord. Don't you wish sometimes that you could have been there too, to receive the Sacred Host directly from Jesus' hands?

Jesus knew we would want that, and this is why He gives His priests the power to stand in His place at the altar, to speak the words that He spoke, and to make present His Body, Blood, Soul and Divinity in each consecrated Host, so that He could come to every single one of us, and stay with us forever.

Every time we go to Mass, Jesus is there with us in the person of the priest. When we hear the bell ring, and the priest lifts up the Sacred Host and the Chalice for all to see, we recall the time that Jesus spoke the same words to create this great miracle for us for the first time. Most of all, we remember that He gave His life for us, and shed His Precious Blood for us on the Cross, offering this perfect sacrifice of Himself to God for all our sins.

Let us, then, always remember to kneel when we see the Cross, and think:

"He loved me and delivered himself for me. All this blood to wash away my sins. What have I done for Him? What am I going to do now? Am I going to sin again?"

Dearest Lord, I love Thee with my whole, whole heart,
Not for what Thou givest, but for what Thou art.
Come, O come, sweet Savior, come to me and stay,
For I want Thee, Jesus, more than I can say.

JESUS INVITES CHILDREN TO HOLY COMMUNION

In the great gift of the Blessed Sacrament, Jesus gives us His very own self! Because this is such a solemn gift, which cost Him so much, sometimes we may feel afraid that we do not deserve such a wonderful gift. And this is true, because nothing we can do can ever make us truly worthy of God. But that is precisely why Jesus came to us and gave us the gift of the Holy Eucharist! The only thing we can offer to God that is worthy of Him is Jesus. So Jesus came to us, and gave us the gift of His Body, so that we might offer Him as a perfect sacrifice to God in the Mass.

It is not only priests and very holy people that may receive Jesus into their hearts. Jesus once said, "Let the little children come unto me, and forbid them not, for of such is the Kingdom of Heaven." And another time He said, "Amen, Amen, I say to you: unless you become as little children, you shall not enter the Kingdom of Heaven." Jesus knew that little children would not be afraid to love Him as He loved them. And so He invites even the little children to receive Him into their hearts.

There are two main things He asks of us when we receive Him in the Eucharist.

First, we must believe that the Sacred Host is truly His Body, just as He told us. In order to believe this, we must learn about Him and the things that He taught us when He was here on Earth. That is why you must learn about our Faith, and about Jesus' promises to us, before your First Communion.

Second, we must have a clean soul to receive Him. We would never want to receive Jesus into a heart that was stained and made ugly with sin. Jesus told a story as a way of explaining this to us. He told the story of a king who gave a great wedding feast. All were invited to the feast, and all who went were happy. But one man came to the feast without the proper wedding garment. When the king saw this man, he was angry. He asked the man why he had not cared enough to wear a wedding garment to the feast, but the man had no answer. And so the king ordered that the man be cast out into the darkness outside.

Jesus our King has invited us all to this great feast of the Holy Eucharist. He has given us the pure white garment for our soul that we must wear to the banquet, through the sacrament of Baptism. We must care for this garment properly. If we are careless and allow our pure white garment to become stained and worn through sin, then we must take time to clean and mend it before we come to the feast of the Holy Eucharist, through the *Sacrament of Penance*. We must confess our sins and be sorry for them. Then when Jesus comes into our hearts, He will find a fitting place prepared for Him.

> Who am I, my Jesus, That Thou com'st to me,
> I have sinned against Thee, often grievously.
> I am very sorry I have caused Thee pain.
> I will never, never wound Thy heart again.

JESUS' MOTHER IS ALSO OUR MOTHER

When Our Lord came to Earth as a little child, He chose the Blessed Virgin Mary to be His Mother and gave her many special graces. She watched over Him with loving care during those years of His infancy and childhood.

Mary is also the mother of all people, and of all children. This is what Jesus Himself wanted. He gave her to us from the cross. Through her help and intercession, we are able to come closer to God and be fit for heaven.

Like all good mothers, Mary wants what is best for us. She also knows that the best thing for us is to love Jesus and to follow His example. See how she holds her Divine Child out to us, saying, "Behold my son who has loved you so much!"

See how He spreads his arms wide and invites us all to come to Him, to receive Him into our hearts so that He may help us to lead a holy life, and to give Him our hearts in return.

Mother of the Infant Jesus
Won't you take me for your child?
Teach me to be like dear Jesus
Pure and humble, sweet and mild.

And while to your heart He nestles,
Will you tell Him I will try
To be good that He may bring me,
Up to God's Home when I die.

TO JESUS THROUGH MARY

When we see Mary, we see her looking to Jesus. In the manger, in the workshop, at the wedding feast at Cana, on the cross, and in the Upper Room at Pentecost, she always looked to Him. After Jesus ascended into heaven, she was mother to His disciples, comforting them and always reminding them of His teachings.

Mary is all these things to us, too. She is always leading us to her Son. She knows what we must do to be good and come to Heaven — we must have Jesus to help us!

Here He is, lying in a beautiful golden vessel in the form of bread and wine, but He is the same Jesus who lay in a manger; the same Jesus who gave Himself to us in the Supper Room and on the Cross. If we receive Him into our hearts every day, just think how much easier it will be for us to become more like Him!

Mother Mary, Mother dear,
Lend thy little Babe to me,
I believe that He is here,
Just the same as on thy knee,
I will kiss His little feet,
Give me Jesus, Mother sweet.

Mother Dear and Mother fair,
Give me Jesus now to hold.
I will take the greatest care,
I will keep Him from the cold.
I will love Him ardently,
Please, O please, give Him to me.

PREPARATION OF THE SOUL: FREE FROM MORTAL SIN

We remember that Jesus asks two things of us in order to receive Him in the Eucharist: First, we must truly believe that it is His Body we are receiving, and second, our soul must be clean and not stained by the ugly spots of Mortal Sin. Let us learn more about what this means.

See the first boy in the picture. He is a good, dear boy who tries always to obey God and obey his parents. You can see this in his heart: it is pure and clean, with no spot of sin. Sometimes he has committed small sins, but he was sorry and confessed them in the *Sacrament of Penance*, so they have been cleaned away. See how happy his guardian angel is! See, too, the rays from heaven that show us that God is pleased with him. He has tried hard to be good, and God loves him.

Now look at the second boy. Is he like the first? His face is clouded and his heart shows the spots of sin. He is still a friend of God, and heaven's light still shines upon him, but he often does not heed the voice of his good angel, who sternly warns him of the danger to his soul.

The devil smiles; he knows that the boy can hear his voice leading him into temptation through anger and pride and greediness. Oh, he must be careful! If he does not try harder to heed the voice of his good angel, he is in danger of becoming like the third boy...

The third boy...oh, look at him! He has chosen to listen to the tempting voice of the devil instead of his good angel, and has fallen into many sins. Just look at the many dark spots on his heart, and the flame of love for God has gone out!

With what sorrow does his Guardian Angel behold this scene! Oh, how he grieves for his dear companion! The light of heaven cannot pierce this boy's soul, shadowed with all those dark spots! Instead of being a friend of God, he has chosen to befriend the enemy of his soul, the devil, who will lead him further and further into sin and away from God!

Which of these boys may receive Jesus in the Holy Eucharist?

Of course the first boy may! He is a true friend of Jesus, with a clean soul. His heart is a welcome place for Jesus to come and stay, and to bring His gifts of grace that will help him to be good and resist temptation.

The second boy may also receive Communion; however, a true friend of Jesus would never wish to invite Him into a heart that is soiled with the dirty spots of sin. First he should tell our Lord he is sorry for his sins through an Act of Contrition. Even better, he should go to Confession, so that those spots may be cleaned away, and make his heart once more a beautiful, clean place for sweet baby Jesus to lie in.

And the third boy? Oh, how he needs the graces that Holy Communion can bring to him! But it would be a very grave sin to invite Jesus into a black heart stained with mortal sin like that. No, he must not do this!

First he must go to Confession and promise to try to change his life and be good. If he is truly sorry for his sins, God will forgive him and restore the life of grace into his soul. This will take the terrible black spots from his heart and make it once more a fitting place for Jesus to come with his gifts of grace in the Eucharist.

How fortunate this boy is, that God has given him a way, through the Sacrament of Penance, to amend his life and make friends once more with Jesus!

How good art Thou, my Jesus dear,
To cleanse my soul from sinful stain,
And make me all Thine own again,
When I repent with heart sincere.

PREPARATION OF THE BODY: THE EUCHARISTIC FAST

Here is James. He lives in the year 1928. James is seven years old and has received his First Communion already. He has learned about Jesus and knows and believes that the Sacred Host is truly Jesus' Body and Blood. He is also careful to keep his soul clean by going to Confession often.

It is Saturday night and James is looking forward to receiving Jesus in Holy Communion tomorrow. He is getting ready to receive Him now.

It is the job of our Holy Mother Church to teach us the proper reverence for Jesus in the Eucharist, and thus she lays upon us a solemn commandment: we must *fast* before receiving Jesus. Her laws regarding this fast vary from place to place, so you must ask your priest for instruction on the current law.

At the time and place where James lived, it was necessary to fast from midnight of the night before receiving Communion. This meant no food, not even water, after midnight. This is sometimes difficult for James, but he loves our Lord and knows that he needs Him to come into his heart and help him to be good. So he gladly makes this sacrifice for Jesus.

During the night, James awakes and is thirsty. But he looks at the clock and sees that it is after midnight. He knows that if he takes a drink, he will not be able to receive Jesus, so he bravely decides to wait. He thinks of Jesus' thirst when he hung on the cross for us. Then he says some prayers and soon falls back to sleep.

Mother wakes James in the morning and he says his morning prayers and gets ready for Mass. As he passes the kitchen table, there is food waiting. It smells good and makes him hungry. But if he eats, he must not receive Jesus, this would be a grave sin. So he will wait. After he has received Jesus, he can have his breakfast.

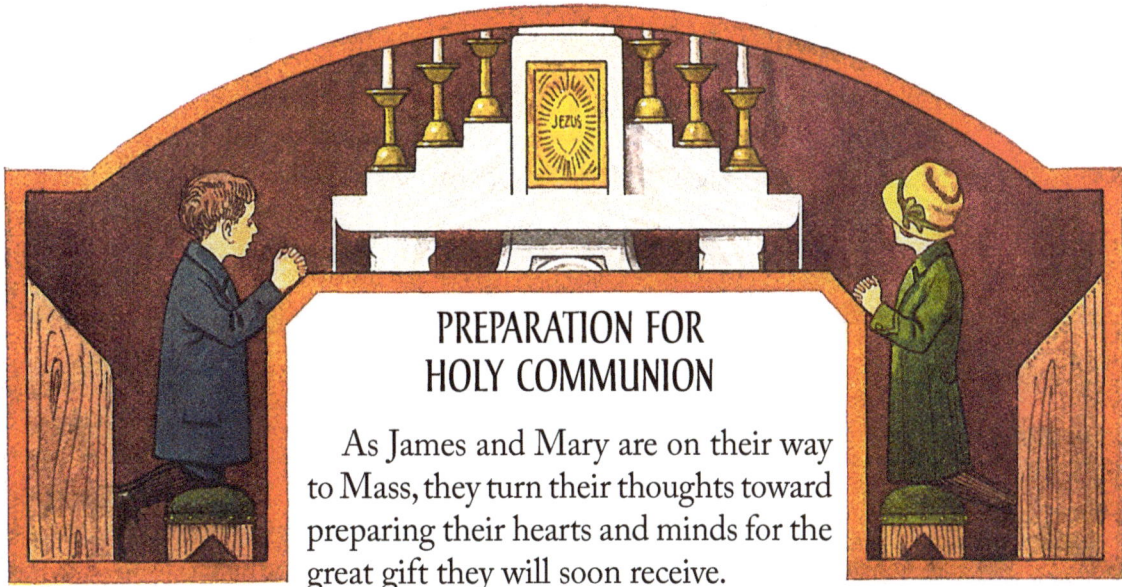

PREPARATION FOR HOLY COMMUNION

As James and Mary are on their way to Mass, they turn their thoughts toward preparing their hearts and minds for the great gift they will soon receive.

All week long they have looked for little ways of showing Jesus their love. They said many extra prayers, in addition to their regular morning and night prayers, and their daily Rosary. They tried very hard to obey their parents promptly. James let Mary have the last cookie, rather than taking it for himself. Mary let James have his way during one of their games, rather than start an argument. All of these things were like sweet-smelling flowers gathered for their King.

At bedtime and upon waking, they turned their thoughts to Jesus and told Him how much they are looking forward to receiving Him.

Jesus, Jesus, come to me
O how much I long for Thee!

They know what a great privilege it is to have Jesus in their hearts, and they have thought about what they wish to ask of Him when He comes. Mary wants to ask Him to help her friend Helen to feel better, for she is ill. James wants to ask Jesus to help him avoid the temptation to argue with one of the boys at school.

On the way to Church, they do not play wildly or make noise. They keep their thoughts focused on Him whom they will soon visit. They arrive at Church in plenty of time to say their acts of Faith, Hope and Love.

When they enter the Church, they must be on their best behavior for a while. They know that someone is there who can help them. There, next to the altar, is a statue of Mary. They will ask for her help.

Mother of Jesus, Mother mine,
Take my little hand in thine.
Lead me where thy Blessed Son
Is waiting for His little one.
Tell Him thou hast brought me here,
To get His blessing, Mother dear.

Jesus, my God, upon my knee,
I worship Thee, I worship Thee.
Thou art great, and wise, and strong,
I am foolish, weak and young.
Clasp me tight and let me rest
My little head upon thy breast.

O dearest Jesus, wilt Thou lie
In my arms a little while
I will hold Thee tenderly,
Look at Thee and Thou wilt smile.
Jesus, Jesus, God and man,
Oh, I will love Thee all I can.

Now, with Mary's help, it is time to turn their full attention to Jesus who is coming. They will now say their acts of Faith, Hope, Love and Contrition.

My God! With heart and soul
and mind, I do in Thee believe,
Because Thou art the very Truth,
that never can deceive.

My God! With heart and soul
and mind, I give my love to Thee,
For Thou art the unfailing love,
the God of charity.

My God! With heart and soul
and mind, I hope in Thee for aye,
For Thou art very Faithfulness,
that never can betray.

My God! With heart and soul
and mind, I grieve for sin's distress,
For Thou, O Truth, O Faith,
O Love, art perfect Holiness!

Jesus, Thou art coming, holy as Thou art,
Thou the God who made me, to my sinful heart.
Jesus, I believe it, on Thy only word,
Kneeling I adore Thee as my King and Lord

Who am I, my Jesus, That Thou com'st to me,
I have sinned against Thee, often grievously.
I am very sorry I have caused Thee pain.
I will never, never wound Thy heart again.

Dearest Lord, I love Thee with my whole, whole heart,
Not for what Thou givest, but for what Thou art.
Come, O come, sweet Savior, come to me and stay,
For I want Thee, Jesus, more than I can say.

COMMUNION TIME

When the time comes, Mary and James approach the Communion Rail. See how they do this with great reverence and respect. They do not slouch or stumble but stand up straight and walk with care, folding their hands together in front of the chest. They keep their heads bowed and eyes cast down out of reverence, and also to avoid the temptation to look around and get distracted.

We can see that Mary and James' angels stand by their sides with love. What we cannot see is what our Lord sees: the beautiful place they have prepared for Him in their hearts! Only Jesus can see that.

James patiently waits for his turn to receive Communion. When he approaches the Communion Rail, he carefully kneels. He then takes in his hands the beautiful white cloth covering the rail, and lifts it gently toward his chest. He does this to help ensure that if the Sacred Host should accidentally fall from the priest's hand, or from his tongue, Our Blessed Lord will not fall upon the floor!

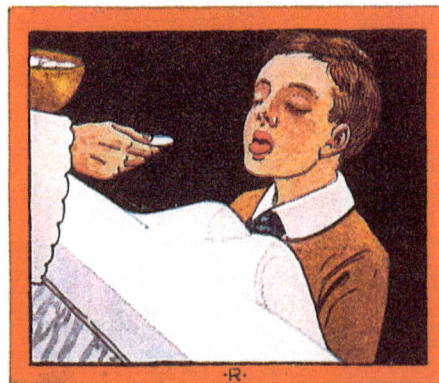

When the priest approaches with the Sacred Host, James lifts his head and tilts it backwards, extending his tongue over his bottom lip to make a place for the Sacred Host. Once the priest places the Host upon his tongue, he slowly and carefully draws it into his mouth and closes it. He lets it remain there a little while to soften, then gently swallows. Oh, what a solemn moment! Jesus has now come into James' heart!

O Jesus dear! O Jesus dear!
I am so glad to hold Thee here;
Although Thou art so weak and small,
Thou art my God, and lord of all.

O babe divine, O babe divine,
Just for a little Thou art mine,
And I can press Thee to my heart,
All great and holy as Thou art.

My brother sweet, my brother sweet,
I kiss Thy tender little feet,
And lay my face against Thy cheek,
And am too happy quite to speak.

O Jesus dear, O Jesus dear,
I want to have Thee always near.
I want my little heart to be
A soft, white cradle-bed for Thee.

THANKSGIVING AFTER COMMUNION

Now that James and Mary carry Jesus in their hearts, they return to their places just as reverently as they approached the communion rail.

How important this moment is! What a privilege and opportunity we have when we receive Jesus! For just a little while, we have Him all to ourselves! We can whisper in His ear and tell Him oh, so many things! And shall we look around and forget to spend this time wisely? Surely not!

Our first task is to greet our Sacred Guest with the adoration and love that are due to our good God, who comes down all the way from Heaven to be with us.

> Thou art my God, Who holdest me,
> I worship Thee, I worship Thee.
> My happy heart is singing low,
> I love Thee so, I love Thee so!

Next we offer Him our thanks, with all the many spiritual gifts we have gathered up for Him during the week.

> Jesus, Lord, how good Thou art,
> To come into my little heart,
> I wish I had some splendid thing,
> to give to Thee, my dearest King.

> I give Thee flow'rs to welcome Thee,
> Sweet Faith and Hope and Charity,
> O Jesus, Lord, how good Thou art,
> To come into my little heart.

We must not neglect contrition for our sins and failings:

> My sorry heart is saying low,
> I wish I had not pained Thee so,
> I want to be quite good to Thee,
> Because Thou art so good to me.

And finally, we present our petitions to our great God and King:

> O bless my lessons
> and my play,
>
> And bless me when
> I kneel to pray,
>
> Bless all who love
> and care for me,
>
> O bless them, Jesus,
> tenderly.

James and Mary's good angels join them in offering their love. We must remember to ask our angels to help us make a good thanksgiving, for they see what we cannot, and know so well how to adore and serve God.

James is doing something very wise: he uses his hands to make a little cave, like the one at Bethlehem where the baby Jesus was born. In order to escape distractions, he will go into his little cave to be alone with Jesus and give all his love and attention only to Him.

Oh, how can we be worthy of such a guest? But what does Jesus ask in return? Does He demand gold or jewels like an earthly king? No, what He asks of us is that we give Him our hearts.

How willingly Mary offers her heart to God, with the help of her good angel and the beautiful verses in her prayer book! She asks our Lord to keep her heart always pure from sin, so that He may live there always, and help her to be a true child of God.

> Ah! What gift or present, Jesus can I bring?
> I have nothing worthy of my God and King.
> But Thou art my Shepherd, I Thy little lamb;
> Take myself, dear Jesus, all I have and am.
>
> Take my body, Jesus, eyes and ears and tongue;
> Never let them, Jesus, help to do Thee wrong.
> Take my heart and fill it full of love for Thee,
> All I have I give Thee, give Thyself to me.

WE OFFER OUR PETITIONS TO GOD

It is very unusual and special to be able to ask favors of an important person like the King or President of a country. Yet when Jesus our King comes to us in Holy Communion, He loves to be asked for the things we want or need. He is not Santa Claus, and He will not bring us everything we want, like toys or money or candy. But if we ask Him to give us the things we truly need to get to Heaven, He will not refuse us. After all, it cost Him so dearly to redeem us by dying on the cross! He who did not hesitate to suffer for our sake will not refuse us the graces we need to be good, if we ask for them earnestly.

But it is not only for ourselves that we ought to pray. It is good and natural that we should wish to pray for our family: our parents, grandparents, brothers and sisters, and our aunts and uncles and cousins. Let us pray that God may bless them in all they do.

Our priest is also like a shepherd who cares for our souls. He needs our prayers, and so do all those who lead and govern God's Church here on earth, especially our bishop and our Holy Father, the Pope. Let us pray that God may guide their steps in the surest way.

Our teachers and our friends also guide us and keep us company along the path to heaven. Let us pray for them, that they may be good examples for us and for others.

Next, we ought to pray for those who cannot pray for themselves, or do not know how — beginning with the Poor Souls in Purgatory, as well as those here on Earth who are weighed down by their sins, and forget or despise God. Oh, how they need our prayers!

We add also those who do not know God, do not believe in Him, or are not baptized. Let us pray that God may bring them closer to Him so that they too may learn to know, love and serve God, and come to heaven someday.

There are many petitions we may offer to God during our time with Him after Communion. When we are done, we should thank Him once more and give Him our love.

⸎⸎

Soon the Mass is ended and it is time to go home. James and Mary behave with reverence as they leave the Church, remembering that they carry Jesus within their hearts now.

Let us leave our dear Lord after Mass with a special prayer, and try to visit Him outside of Mass when we can.

I wish I were the little key
That locks Love's Captive in,
And lets Him out to go and free
A sinful heart from sin.

I wish I were the little bell
That tinkles for the Host,
When God comes down each day to dwell
With hearts He loves the most.

I wish I were the chalice fair,
That holds the Blood of Love,
When every flash lights holy prayer
Upon its way above.

I wish I were the little flower
So near the Host's sweet face,
Or like the light that half an hour
Burns on the shrine of grace.

I wish I were the altar where,
As on His mother's breast,
Christ nestles, like a child, fore'er
In Eucharistic rest.

But, oh! My God, I wish the most
That my poor heart may be
A home all holy for each Host
That comes in love to me.

EDITOR'S NOTE:

This book began its life as *Het Prentenboek van de Eerste H. Communie*, a book written in the 1920s by Brother Maria Cassianus Versteeg (1884-1956). He was a member of a religious community in the Netherlands which operated schools in Den Bosch and Tilburg, as well as a boys orphanage. In order to help support themselves, as well as to create opportunities for the orphaned boys to learn a useful trade, the Brothers set up a printing house in Tilburg. This highly successful and influential press, called the *Drukkerij van het RK Jongensweeshuis,* printed more than 11,000 titles over the course of its existence between 1846 and 1959. Most were children's books, both recreational and educational, some of which have since become sought-after collectibles. Many of these books were imaginatively illustrated by Bernard Reith, whose prolific work began with comic books and included regular contributions to the Dutch Catholic weekly magazine, *Catholic Illustration.*

We discovered this book and its companion *Het Prentenboek van de Kinderbiecht* (My Picture Book of First Confession) thanks to its marvelous illustrations. However, in the process of translating it from the original Dutch, we found the text to be less than ideal. (We wondered whether perhaps it was written with the intention of scaring the orphanage boys into behaving?) Nevertheless, the illustrations alone were so compelling that we chose to persevere...even if that meant completely rewriting the text to accompany them.

Of course, it would be rather incongruous to have illustrations like these alongside a modern 21st-century text. So we relied heavily on the work of Mother Mary Loyola, our favorite author, who would have been alive at the time these books were originally published. It is for this reason that I do not claim authorship of these two books; using a basic outline derived from a rough translation of the original Dutch, I borrowed heavily from Mother Loyola, so I prefer to say only that I *adapted* and *edited* this book, based on the original by M.C. Versteeg.

In Christ,
Lisa Bergman
St. Augustine Academy Press
Feast of the Nativity of the B.V.M.

©2020 by St. Augustine Academy Press
ISBN: 978-1-64051-083-8

Nihil Obstat:
Reverend Scott McCawley
Censor Deputatus
September 1, 2020

Imprimatur:
Most Reverend Richard E. Pates
Apostolic Administrator
Diocese of Joliet
September 1, 2020

The *Nihil Obstat* and *Imprimatur* are official declarations that a book is free of doctrinal and moral error. No implication is contained therein that those who have granted the *Nihil Obstat* and *Imprimatur* agree with the content, opinions, or statements expressed. Nor do they assume legal responsibility associated with publication.

www.ingramcontent.com/pod-product-compliance
Lightning Source LLC
Chambersburg PA
CBHW040857100426

42813CB00015B/2833